# COO

## HOW TO MIL

*BY*

## "BERNARD"


LONDON

## W. FOULSHAM & CO., LTD.

NEW YORK   TORONTO   CAPE TOWN   SYDNEY

*W. FOULSHAM & CO. LTD.*
*Yeovil Road, Slough, Bucks, England.*

ISBN 0-572-00184-3

MADE IN GREAT BRITAIN
BY JOHN GARDNER (PRINTERS) LTD., LIVERPOOL, 20
© W. FOULSHAM & CO. LTD. 1970.

# CONTENTS

# PREFACE

THE writer of this book has, for many years, made a habit of jotting down the recipe of every cocktail, that he has come across, which possessed special merit. The present compilation of well over a hundred recipes is the result of his notes.

As he has travelled in various parts of the world and has gathered the recipes from far and wide, the collection is more or less unique.

# 100 COCKTAILS
# HOW TO MIX THEM

## SECTION I
## COCKTAILS

*(All of which are Alcoholic)*

How the dictionaries define a cocktail, I do not know; but, were I asked, I should say that it was a delicate combination of ingredients, all of which contribute their share in building up a unique beverage, possessing an individualism of its own.

Whether the reader agrees with me or not hardly matters. What does matter is that he should appreciate that the ingredients of a cocktail have been thought out and selected by a master-mind who has blended them together to obtain a definite flavour. Thus, to alter them, in substance or quantity, will surely alter the resulting effect—and, generally, an alteration means an inferior result.

Having stressed the need for keeping faithfully to the recipes, as printed, the next point to note is that it is advisable to put the ingredients together in the order they figure in the recipes. Sometimes it is essential and, if the habit is formed, there will never be any mistakes.

For your cocktail bar, a certain number of implements are, more or less, necessary. They may be enumerated as follows :

1. *A Shaker*. This consists of two metal plated containers which fit one in the other. The contrivance is held in both hands and shaken up and down until the ingredients are thoroughly mixed.

Other types of shakers, for which it was claimed no ice was needed, have appeared on the market, but presumably were not successful, since they are no longer attainable.

2. *A Strainer*. This is composed of a metal ring, covered with gauze, and a handle attached. After the ingredients have been shaken or stirred, the mixture is poured through it to strain out the chips of ice, fruit pulp, etc.

3. *A Mixing Glass*. This is merely a large tumbler or bar-glass, into which the ingredients are put when they are to be stirred. Note, here, that some liquids, such as champagne, must not be shaken or they will lose their natural effervescence. Such liquids are stirred in the mixing glass.

4. *A Mixing Spoon*. This is a spoon holding about the same amount as a teaspoon, but with a very long handle. It makes stirring easy.

5. *A Gill Measure*. It should be graded to permit of the measuring of such fractions as $\frac{1}{2}$, $\frac{1}{3}$, $\frac{1}{4}$, $\frac{1}{6}$, etc., gills.

6. *A Bundle of Cherry Sticks* to permit of the simple manipulation of cherries, olives, etc., which are often served with cocktails.

7. *A Supply of Drinking Straws*.

8. *A Corkscrew and Bottle Opener*.

Though the above outfit is required for any cocktail bar, there are certain things needed far more, and they are the drinks themselves. A well-appointed bar should stock the following :—

| | |
|---|---|
| *Absinthe.* | *Grenadine Syrup.* |
| *Angostura Bitters.* | *Italian Vermouth.* |
| *Brandy.* | *Maraschino.* |
| *Brown Curaçao.* | *Orange Bitters.* |
| *Calvados.* | *Plain Syrup.* |
| *Canadian Club Whisky.* | *Red Port.* |
| *Champagne.* | *Rum.* |
| *Dubonnet.* | *Scotch Whisky.* |
| *French Vermouth.* | *Sherry.* |
| *Gin.* | |

With the above ingredients on hand, ninety per cent. of the alcoholic recipes in this

book can be compounded, if such oddments as
sprigs of mint and cherries are not counted.

Now a word about the glasses in which the
drinks should be served :—

1. *A Cocktail Glass* holds about ½ gill of
liquid.

2. *A Small Wine Glass* holds about ¾ gill.

3. *A Large Wine Glass* holds about 1 gill.

4. *A Tumbler* holds about ½ pint, which is
2 gills.

5. *A Sherbet Glass* is like a small tumbler.

6. *A Liqueur Glass* holds about ¼ gill.

7. *A Sundae Glass* is bowl-shaped and is
useful when serving fruit cocktails.

And, while mentioning gills and things, it
may be useful to add, in case you have for-
gotten, that

> 4 *gills* make 1 *pint*.
> 2 *pints* ,, 1 *quart*.
> 4 *quarts* ,, 1 *gallon*.

## ABSINTHE COCKTAIL

¼ *gill of Absinthe.*
1 *dash of Angostura Bitters.*
2 *dashes of Anisette (or Plain Syrup).*
1 *dash of Lemon Peel Juice.*
⅛ *gill of Water.*
1 *Cherry.*
¾ *tumbler of broken Ice.*

Three-quarters fill a tumbler with broken ice and add the Angostura Bitters. Then put in the Absinthe, the Anisette, and the Water. Shake well and pass through a strainer into a cocktail glass. Serve with a dash of lemon peel juice on top and with a cherry.

For anyone who knows little of cocktails, this is an excellent one to try at the outset.

### ADAM'S APPLE COCKTAIL

> ¼ *gill of Calvados.*
> ⅛ *gill of Italian Vermouth.*
> ⅛ *gill of Gin.*
> 2 *dashes of Yellow Chartreuse.*
> 1 *Dash of Lemon Peel Juice.*
> 1 *Cherry.*
> ½ *tumblerful of broken Ice.*

Half fill a tumbler with broken ice. Then add the Calvados, the Italian Vermouth, the Gin and the Yellow Chartreuse. Stir well and pass through a strainer into a cocktail glass. Serve with a cherry and a dash of lemon peel juice on top.

A fairly strong cocktail.

### ALCAZAR COCKTAIL

> ⅙ *gill of Bénédictine.*
> ¼ *gill of Canadian Club Whisky.*
> 1 or 2 *dashes of Orange Peel Juice.*
> 1 *Cherry.*
> ½ *tumblerful of broken Ice.*

Half fill a tumbler with broken ice. Then add
the Canadian Club Whisky and the Bénédictine. Stir well and pass through a strainer
into a cocktail glass. Serve with a cherry and
a dash of orange peel juice on top.

If desired, a small dash of Orange Bitters
may be included in the above.

## APPLEJACK COCKTAIL

⅓ *Gill of Calvados.*
1 *dash of Angostura Bitters.*
1 *teaspoonful of Brown Curaçao.*
½ *tumblerful of broken Ice.*
1 *Cherry.*
1 *dash of Lemon Peel Juice.*

Half fill the tumbler with broken ice and add
the Angostura Bitters. Then add the Calvados
and the Brown Curaçao. Stir up and pass
through a strainer into a cocktail glass. Serve
with a cherry and a dash of lemon peel juice
on top.

Orange Bitters can be used instead of
Angostura Bitters, if preferred.

Calvados is the continental name for
Applejack Brandy.

## BACARDI COCKTAIL

¼ *gill of Bacardi.*
¼ *gill of Lime Juice.*
2 *dashes of Grenadine Syrup.*
1 *Cherry.*
¼ *tumblerful of broken Ice.*

Half fill the tumbler with broken ice and add the Bacardi. Then add the Lime juice and the Grenadine Syrup. Stir well and pass through a strainer into a cocktail glass. Serve with a cherry.

A very pleasant cocktail. This drink is very popular in America.

### BAMBOO COCKTAIL—1

$\frac{1}{4}$ *gill of Dry Sherry.*
$\frac{1}{4}$ *gill of French Vermouth.*
$\frac{1}{2}$ *teaspoonful of Orange Bitters.*
1 *dash of Lemon Peel Juice.*
$\frac{1}{2}$ *tumblerful of broken Ice.*

Half fill a tumbler with broken ice and add the Orange Bitters. Then add the Dry Sherry and the French Vermouth. Stir well, strain and serve in a cocktail glass with a dash of lemon peel juice on top.

### BAMBOO COCKTAIL—2

$\frac{1}{3}$ *gill of Dry Sherry.*
$\frac{1}{6}$ *gill of Italian Vermouth.*
$\frac{1}{2}$ *teaspoonful of Orange Bitters.*
1 *dash of Lemon Peel Juice.*
$\frac{1}{2}$ *tumblerful of broken Ice.*

This cocktail is made up in exactly the same way as the previous one ; but Italian Vermouth is used instead of French Vermouth. This makes the flavour much sweeter and, in our experience, it is preferred by women-folk.

### BENNETT COCKTAIL

⅓ *gill of Gin.*
⅙ *gill of Lemon (or Lime) Juice.*
1 *teaspoonful of Angostura Bitters.*
½ *shakerful of broken Ice.*

Half fill the shaker with broken ice and add the Gin. Then add the lemon (or lime) juice and the Angostura Bitters. Shake well and pass through a strainer into a cocktail glass.

This drink is very popular in South America.

### BEVERLY HILLS COCKTAIL

½ *gill of Calvados.*
2 *dashes of Angostura Bitters.*
1 *dash of Lemon Peel Juice.*
1 *Cherry.*
½ *tumblerful of broken Ice.*

The tumbler is half filled with broken ice and the Angostura Bitters added. Then add the Calvados. Stir well and pass through a strainer into a cocktail glass. Serve with a cherry and a dash of lemon peel juice on top.

This cocktail is named after the famous town near Hollywood, California.

### BIG BOY COCKTAIL

⅛ *gill of French Vermouth.*
⅛ *gill of Italian Vermouth.*
¼ *gill of Gin.*

1 *teaspoonful of Angostura Bitters.*
1 *teaspoonful of Absinthe.*
1 *dash of Lemon Peel Juice.*
1 *Cherry.*
½ *tumblerful of broken Ice.*

Half fill the tumbler with broken ice and add the Angostura Bitters. Then add the French Vermouth, the Italian Vermouth, the Gin and the Absinthe. Stir up and pass through a strainer into a cocktail glass. Serve with a cherry and a dash of lemon peel juice on top.

A very pleasant cocktail which is, also, fairly strong.

## BIJOU COCKTAIL

⅛ *gill of Dry Gin.*
⅛ *gill of Green Chartreuse.*
⅛ *gill of Italian Vermouth.*
½ *teaspoonful of Orange Bitters.*
1 *dash of Lemon Peel Juice.*
1 *Cherry.*
½ *tumblerful of broken Ice.*

Half fill a tumbler with broken ice and add the Dry Gin. Then add the Chartreuse, the Italian Vermouth and the Orange Bitters. Stir well and pass through a strainer into a cocktail glass. Serve with a dash of lemon peel juice on top and with a cherry.

For those who enjoy something mild.

Some people prefer to leave out the Orange Bitters.

### BLACKTHORN COCKTAIL—1

1 *teaspoonful of Absinthe.*
½ *teaspoonful of Angostura Bitters.*
¼ *gill of French Vermouth.*
¼ *gill of Scotch Whisky.*
1 *dash of Lemon Peel Juice.*
½ *tumblerful of broken Ice.*

Half fill a tumbler with broken ice and add the Absinthe. Then add the Angostura Bitters, the French Vermouth and the Scotch Whisky. Stir well and pass through a strainer into a wine glass. Serve with a dash of lemon peel juice on top.

### BLACKTHORN COCKTAIL—2

½ *teaspoonful of Orange Bitters.*
1 *dash of Angostura Bitters.*
⅙ *gill of Scotch Whisky.*
⅙ *gill of French Vermouth.*
⅙ *gill of Italian Vermouth.*
1 *Cherry.*
½ *tumblerful of broken Ice.*

This cocktail is made up in the same way as the previous one except that Orange Bitters and Italian Vermouth are added and the Absinthe is left out.

The flavour is not quite so subtle as the previous one, but it is an excellent alternative for those people who do not appreciate the taste of Absinthe.

### BLACKTHORN COCKTAIL—3

1 *dash of Angostura Bitters.*
1 *dash of Orange Bitters.*
⅙ *gill of Italian Vermouth.*
⅓ *gill of Sloe Gin.*
1 *dash of Lemon Peel Juice.*
½ *tumblerful of broken Ice.*

Make up as in the previous case. Sloe Gin is used in place of the Scotch Whisky and the French Vermouth is left out.

A more mellow flavour than the previous.

### BRANDY COCKTAIL—1

1 *dash of Absinthe.*
10 *drops of Angostura Bitters.*
1 *teaspoonful of Brown Curaçao.*
⅓ *gill of brandy.*
1 *dash of Lemon Peel Juice.*
1 *Cherry.*
½ *tumblerful of broken Ice.*

Half fill the tumbler with ice chips and add the dash of Absinthe. Next add the Angostura Bitters, the Curaçao and the Brandy. Stir well and pass through a strainer into a cocktail glass. Serve with a cherry and a dash of lemon peel juice on top.

## BRANDY COCKTAIL—2

¼ *gill of Brandy.*
¼ *gill of French Vermouth.*
1 *dash of Lemon Peel Juice.*
1 *Cherry.*
½ *tumblerful of broken Ice.*

This cocktail is made up in exactly the same way as the previous one. Use French Vermouth instead of the Absinthe, the Angostura Bitters, and the Curaçao. This makes a delightful variation.

A simpler cocktail to make than the previous one and, therefore, it will be appreciated on occasion.

## BRAZIL COCKTAIL

¼ *gill of Dry Sherry.*
¼ *gill of French Vermouth.*
1 *dash of Orange Bitters.*
2 *dashes of Absinthe.*
1 *dash of Plain Syrup.*
1 *dash of Lemon Peel Juice.*
½ *tumblerful of broken Ice.*

The tumbler is half filled with broken ice and the Orange Bitters added. Then add the Dry Sherry, the French Vermouth, the Plain Syrup and the Absinthe. Stir well, strain and serve in a cocktail or small wine glass with a dash of lemon peel juice on top.

This is a very pleasant cocktail of medium strength.

## BROADWAY COCKTAIL

*A few drops of Orange Bitters.*
*½ gill of Italian Vermouth.*
*½ gill of Dry Gin.*
*1 dash of Orange Peel Juice.*
*½ shakerful of broken Ice.*

Half fill the shaker with broken ice and add the Orange Bitters. Then put in the Italian Vermouth and the Dry Gin. Shake well and pass through a strainer into a small wine glass. Serve with a dash of orange peel juice on top.

This cocktail is very popular in New York.

## BRONX COCKTAIL

*$\frac{1}{1\frac{1}{2}}$ gill of Italian Vermouth.*
*$\frac{1}{1\frac{1}{2}}$ gill of French Vermouth.*
*⅛ gill of Dry Gin.*
*1 dash of Orange Bitters.*
*1 tablespoonful of Orange Juice.*
*½ shakerful of broken Ice.*

Half fill the shaker with broken ice and then, in the following order, put in the Dry Gin, the Italian Vermouth, the French Vermouth, the Orange Juice and the Orange Bitters. Shake well and pass through a strainer into a cocktail glass.

Some connoisseurs prefer the above without the Orange Bitters. They say that it gives a smoother flavour.

## BUZZER COCKTAIL

¼ *gill of Dry Gin.*
¼ *gill of Italian Vermouth.*
1 *teaspoonful of Crème de Menthe.*
2 *dashes of Angostura Bitters.*
1 *Cherry.*
½ *shakerful of broken Ice.*

The shaker is half filled with broken ice and
the Angostura Bitters added. Then add the
Dry Gin, the Italian Vermouth and the Crème
de Menthe. Shake well and pass through a
strainer into a cocktail glass. Serve with a
cherry.

A pleasant and fairly strong cocktail.

## CHAMPAGNE COCKTAIL—1

1 *gill of Champagne.*
*A few drops of Brown Curaçao.*
*A few drops of Old Brandy.*
*A few drops of Plain Syrup.*

When making this or any other Champagne
cocktail be careful to have a bottle of Champagne on ice, and to keep it well corked.
About 6 to 8 cocktails can be made with a bottle
of Champagne.

An ordinary wine glass is best for measuring the drink. It is prepared in a tumbler
half filled with broken ice. Add the
Curaçao, the Old Brandy, the Plain Syrup and
the Champagne in the above order. Stir
well and serve in a large wine glass.

### CHAMPAGNE COCKTAIL—2

> 3 or 4 *dashes of Angostura Bitters.*
> ¾ *gill of Champagne.*
> 1 *slice of Lemon.*
> The juice of ¼ *Lemon.*
> 1 *small lump of Sugar.*
> 1 *small piece of Ice.*

Soak the lump of sugar in the Angostura Bitters. Squeeze the juice of ¼ lemon into a wine glass and add the saturated sugar. Then add the piece of ice and fill up with the Champagne. Serve with a slice of lemon.

This is an admirable pick-me-up.

### CHEERIO COCKTAIL

> 1/12 *gill of Italian Vermouth.*
> 1/12 *gill of French Vermouth.*
> ⅙ *gill of Dry Gin.*
> 2 *dashes of Absinthe.*
> 1 *dash of Orange Bitters.*
> 1 *tablespoonful of Orange Juice.*
> ½ *shakerful of broken Ice.*

Half fill the shaker with broken ice and add the Orange Bitters. Then add the Orange Juice, the Italian Vermouth, the French Vermouth, the Dry Gin and the Absinthe. Shake well and pass through a strainer into a cocktail glass.

Many people prefer to add the Absinthe afterwards and not to put it in the shaker.

Tangerine juice can be used instead of Orange juice. This makes a pleasant variation.

## CHERRY WHISKY

½ teaspoonful of Angostura Bitters.
1 teaspoonful of Grenadine Syrup.
½ gill of Scotch Whisky.
1 dash of Lemon Peel Juice.
1 Cherry.
½ tumblerful of broken Ice.

The tumbler is half filled with broken ice and the Angostura Bitters is added. Then add the Grenadine Syrup and the Whisky. Stir well and pass through a strainer into a wine glass. Serve with a cherry and a dash of lemon peel juice on top.

## CHICAGO COCKTAIL

A few drops of Angostura Bitters.
1 or 2 dashes of Brown Curaçao.
¼ gill of Brandy.
¼ gill of Champagne.
1 dash of Lemon Juice.
1 piece of Lemon Peel.
1 teaspoonful of powdered Sugar.
⅓ tumblerful of broken Ice.

Half fill a tumbler with broken ice and add the Angostura Bitters. Next add the Curaçao, the Brandy and the Champagne. Stir well. Before serving, moisten the inside of a cocktail glass with the lemon peel and sprinkle with sugar. Then strain the mixture into the cocktail glass and serve with a small piece of lemon peel on top.

## CHOCOLATE COCKTAIL

*¼ gill of Red Port.*
*The yolk of a fresh Egg.*
*1 teaspoonful of Chocolate Powder.*
*½ tumblerful of broken Ice.*

Half fill a tumbler with broken ice and add the yolk of an egg. Then add the Red Port and the chocolate powder. Stir well and pass through a strainer into a wine glass.

Some people like to add 1 or 2 dashes of Yellow Chartreuse as well; but this is entirely optional.

## CLOVER CLUB COCKTAIL—1

*½ gill of Dry Gin.*
*1 teaspoonful of Grenadine Syrup.*
*The juice of a Lemon.*
*The white of an Egg.*
*1 dash of Nutmeg.*
*½ shakerful of broken Ice.*

Half fill the shaker with broken ice and add the white of an egg. Then add the lemon juice, the Grenadine Syrup and the Dry Gin. Shake well and pass through a strainer into a cocktail glass containing a dash of nutmeg.

Raspberry Syrup can be used instead of Grenadine Syrup, if desired. Be careful not to over-do the nutmeg.

## CLOVER CLUB COCKTAIL—2

¼ *gill of Dry Gin.*
⅛ *gill of French Vermouth.*
1 *teaspoonful of Grenadine Syrup.*
*The juice of a Lemon.*
*The white of an Egg.*
½ *shakerful of broken Ice.*

This cocktail is made in exactly the same way as the previous one but with the addition of ⅛ gill of French Vermouth. This makes the cocktail much drier.

See also Royal Clover Club cocktail.

## CLOVER LEAF COCKTAIL

½ *gill of Dry Gin.*
1 *teaspoonful of Grenadine Syrup.*
*The juice of a Lemon.*
*The white of an Egg.*
2 *sprigs of Mint.*
½ *shakerful of broken Ice.*

This is much the same as the Clover Club cocktails, but the sprigs of mint make a subtle difference to the flavour.

## CLUB COCKTAIL

12 *drops of Angostura Bitters.*
⅓ *gill of Canadian Club Whisky.*
1 *dash of Grenadine.*
1 *dash of Lemon Peel Juice.*
1 *Cherry.*
¾ *tumblerful of broken Ice.*

A tumbler is half filled with broken ice and the Angostura Bitters is added. Then add the Grenadine and the Canadian Club Whisky. Stir well and pass through a strainer into a cocktail glass. Serve with a cherry and a dash of lemon peel juice.

This cocktail is very popular and is of medium strength.

### COFFEE COCKTAIL

> ½ *teaspoonful of Sugar.*
> ¼ *gill of Port.*
> ⅛ *gill of Brandy.*
> *The yolk of an Egg.*
> ½ *shakerful of Ice.*

Half fill the shaker with ice chips and add the yolk of an egg. Then add the sugar, the Port and the Brandy. Shake till cold and pass through a strainer into a wine glass.

This cocktail is quite mild in flavour. It is a favourite with our women-folk.

### COOPERSTOWN COCKTAIL—1

> ½ *gill of Dry Gin.*
> ⅙ *gill of Italian Vermouth.*
> ½ *teaspoonful of Orange Bitters.*
> 1 *or* 2 *dashes of Lemon Peel Juice.*
> 2 *or* 3 *sprigs of Mint.*
> ½ *tumblerful of broken Ice.*

Half fill the tumbler with ice chips and add the Dry Gin. Then add the Italian Vermouth,

the Orange Bitters, and the sprigs of mint.
Stir well and pass through a strainer into a
cocktail glass. Serve with 1 or 2 dashes of
lemon peel juice on top.

## COOPERSTOWN COCKTAIL—2

⅛ *gill of French Vermouth.*
⅛ *gill of Italian Vermouth*
¼ *gill of Dry Gin.*
2 *or* 3 *sprigs of Mint.*
1 *or* 2 *dashes of Lemon Peel Juice.*
½ *tumblerful of broken Ice.*

This cocktail is much the same as the previous
recipe, but French Vermouth is used to obtain
a drier flavour. The Orange Bitters is
omitted.

## CORONATION COCKTAIL—1

⅓ *gill of Old Brandy.*
2 *teaspoonfuls of Red Curaçao.*
1 *teaspoonful of Peach Bitters.*
1 *teaspoonful of Peppermint.*
1 *slice of Lemon.*
½ *tumblerful of broken Ice.*

Half fill a tumbler with broken ice. Put in the
following order the Peppermint, the Peach
Bitters, the Curaçao, and the Brandy. Stir
well and pass through a strainer into a cocktail
glass. Serve with a slice of lemon on top.

Reduce the quantity of Curaçao, if a cocktail of medium strength is preferred.

## CORONATION COCKTAIL—2

> ¼ *gill of French Vermouth.*
> ¼ *gill of Sherry.*
> 1 *teaspoonful of Angostura Bitters.*
> 1 *teaspoonful of Maraschino.*
> ½ *shakerful of broken ice.*

Half fill the shaker with broken ice and add the French Vermouth. Then add the Sherry, the Maraschino, and the Angostura Bitters. Shake well and strain into a cocktail glass.

Some experts add Dubonnet instead of the Angostura Bitters and Maraschino. It provides a good variation and makes an excellent *apéritif.*

## DAIQUIRI COCKTAIL

> ⅓ *gill of Lime Juice.*
> 1 *or 2 dashes of Grenadine.*
> ⅙ *gill of Rum.*
> ½ *shakerful of broken Ice.*

Half fill the shaker with broken ice and add the Lime juice. Then add the Rum and the Grenadine. Shake well and pass through a strainer into a cocktail glass.

This is quite a mild cocktail.

### DAYDREAM COCKTAIL

1 *teaspoonful of Brown Curaçao.*
1 *teaspoonful of Angostura Bitters.*
⅓ *gill of Brandy.*
1 *teaspoonful of Maraschino.*
1 *dash of Champagne.*
1 *dash of Lemon Peel Juice.*
1 *Cherry.*
½ *tumblerful of broken Ice.*

Half fill the tumbler with broken ice and add
the Curaçao. Then put in the Angostura
Bitters, the Brandy and the Maraschino. Stir
well and pass through a strainer into a cocktail
glass. Serve with a dash of Champagne, a
dash of lemon peel juice and a cherry.

Pineapple Syrup can be used instead of
Maraschino, if desired.

### DEAUVILLE COCKTAIL

½ *gill of Dry Gin.*
2 *dashes of Plain Syrup.*
2 *dashes of Lime Juice.*
1 *dash of Lemon Peel Juice.*
½ *shakerful of broken Ice.*

Half fill the shaker with broken ice and add the
Dry Gin. Then add the Lime juice and the
Plain Syrup. Shake well and pass through a
strainer into a cocktail glass. Serve with a
dash of lemon peel juice on top.

This cocktail is very popular with the fair sex.

### DEEP SEA COCKTAIL

¼ *gill of Dry Gin.*
¼ *gill of French Vermouth.*
½ *teaspoonful of Absinthe.*
½ *teaspoonful of Orange Bitters.*
1 *dash of Lemon Peel Juice.*
1 *Olive.*
½ *shakerful of Ice chips.*

The shaker is half filled with ice chips and the Dry Gin added. Then add the French Vermouth, the Absinthe and the Orange Bitters. Shake well and pass through a strainer into a small wine glass. Serve with an olive and a dash of lemon peel juice on top.

This cocktail is of medium strength.

### DEMPSEY COCKTAIL

½ *teaspoonful of Absinthe.*
1 *dash of Grenadine.*
⅓ *gill of Brandy.*
⅙ *gill of Dry Gin.*
½ *shakerful of broken Ice.*

Half fill the shaker with broken ice and add the Absinthe. Then put in the Grenadine, the Brandy and the Gin. Shake up and pass through a strainer into a cocktail glass.

A cocktail with plenty of " kick " in it.

## DEVIL'S COCKTAIL

⅙ *gill of Peppermint.*
⅓ *gill of Old Brandy.*
½ *shakerful of broken Ice.*

Half fill the shaker with broken ice and add the Peppermint. Then add the Brandy. Shake up and pass through a strainer into a cocktail glass.

This cocktail is quite strong. Not for beginners.

## DIABOLO COCKTAIL

⅛ *gill of Brown Curaçao.*
⅛ *gill of French Vermouth.*
¼ *gill of Brandy.*
½ *teaspoonful of Angostura Bitters.*
1 *dash of Lemon Peel Juice.*
1 *Cherry.*
½ *tumblerful of broken Ice.*

Half fill the tumbler with the broken ice and add the Curaçao. Then add the French Vermouth, the Brandy and the Angostura Bitters. Shake well and pass through a strainer into a cocktail glass. Serve with a cherry and a dash of lemon peel juice.

This cocktail has plenty of " kick " in it.

## DIAMOND COCKTAIL

⅙ *gill of Rum.*
⅙ *gill of Gin.*
⅙ *gill of Brown Curaçao.*
1 *dash of Lemon Peel Juice.*
½ *tumblerful of broken Ice.*

The tumbler should be half filled with broken ice and the Rum added. Then add the Gin and the Brown Curaçao. Shake well and strain into a cocktail glass. Serve with a dash of lemon peel juice.

A fairly strong cocktail. It is not everybody's choice.

## DIPLOMAT COCKTAIL

⅛ *gill of Italian Vermouth.*
¼ *gill of French Vermouth*
⅛ *gill of Pineapple Syrup.*
1 *dash of Lemon Peel Juice.*
1 *Cherry.*
½ *tumblerful of broken Ice.*

Half fill the tumbler with broken ice and add the French Vermouth. Then add the Italian Vermouth and the Pineapple Syrup. Stir up and pass through a strainer into a cocktail glass. Serve with a dash of lemon peel juice and a cherry.

A fairly mild cocktail.

## DUBONNET COCKTAIL

$\frac{1}{3}$ *gill of Dubonnet.*
$\frac{1}{6}$ *gill of Dry Gin.*
$\frac{1}{2}$ *teaspoonful of Orange Bitters.*
$\frac{1}{2}$ *shakerful of broken Ice.*

The shaker is half filled with broken ice and the Dry Gin is added.   Next add the Dubonnet and the Orange Bitters.   Shake up and pass through a strainer into a cocktail glass.

This is a very good *apéritif.*

### FIOUPE COCKTAIL

$\frac{1}{6}$ *gill of Brandy.*
$\frac{1}{6}$ *gill of Italian Vermouth.*
2 *or* 3 *dashes of Bénédictine.*
1 *or* 2 *dashes of Lemon Peel Juice.*
1 *Cherry.*
$\frac{1}{2}$ *tumblerful of broken Ice.*

Half fill the tumbler with broken ice and add the Brandy.   Next add the Italian Vermouth and the Bénédictine.   Stir up and pass through a strainer into a cocktail glass.   Serve with a cherry and 1 or 2 dashes of lemon peel juice on top.

This cocktail has plenty of " kick " in it.

### FIRE DEVIL COCKTAIL

¼ gill of Sloe Gin.
⅑ gill of French Vermouth.
⅑ gill of Italian Vermouth.
2 dashes of Angostura Bitters.
1 dash of Lemon Peel Juice.
½ tumblerful of broken Ice.

The tumbler is half filled with broken ice and the Angostura Bitters added. Now put in the Sloe Gin, the French Vermouth and the Italian Vermouth. Stir up and pass through a strainer into a cocktail glass. Serve with a dash of lemon peel juice on top.

Using Peach or Orange Bitters makes a pleasant variation.

### FLASH COCKTAIL

½ gill of Gin.
1 teaspoonful of Angostura Bitters.
1 teaspoonful of Absinthe.
1 Cherry.
1 dash of Lemon Peel Juice.
½ shakerful of broken Ice.

Half fill the shaker with broken ice and add the Angostura Bitters. Then add the Gin and the Absinthe. Shake up and strain into a cocktail glass. Serve with a cherry and a dash of lemon peel juice.

Anisette may be used in place of Absinthe, if desired. This makes a delightful variation.

3—C

## FLORIDA COCKTAIL

$\frac{1}{4}$ *gill of Angostura Bitters.*
1 *dash of Plain Syrup.*
*The juice of* $\frac{1}{4}$ *Lemon.*
*The juice of* $\frac{1}{4}$ *Orange.*
1 *dash of Lemon Peel Juice.*
1 *Cherry.*
$\frac{1}{2}$ *shakerful of broken Ice.*

Half fill the shaker with broken ice and add the Angostura Bitters. Then put in the lemon juice, the orange juice and the Plain Syrup. Shake well and strain into a cocktail glass. Serve with a cherry and a dash of lemon peel juice on top.

This is a cocktail of medium strength.

## GANGSTER COCKTAIL

$\frac{1}{4}$ *gill of Brandy.*
$\frac{1}{4}$ *gill of Brown Curaçao.*
1 *dash of Lemon Peel Juice.*
1 *Cherry.*
$\frac{1}{2}$ *shakerful of broken Ice.*

Half fill the shaker with broken ice. Then put in the Brandy and the Brown Curaçao. Shake well and pass through a strainer into a cocktail glass. Serve with a cherry and a dash of lemon peel juice.

This is quite a strong cocktail and should not be drunk on an empty stomach.

## GIBSON COCKTAIL

½ gill of Dry Gin.
½ gill of French Vermouth.
1 small piece of Garlic.
½ tumblerful of broken Ice.

The tumbler is half filled with broken ice and
the Dry Gin is added. Now put in the
French Vermouth. Stir well. Smear the
inside of the cocktail glass with the garlic and
then strain the mixture into it.

This is a dry cocktail. Be very sparing
with the garlic or the whole flavour of the
cocktail will be masked.

## GIN COCKTAIL

⅛ gill of Gin.
1 dash of Angostura Bitters.
2 dashes of Brown Curaçao.
1 dash of Lemon Peel Juice.
1 Cherry.
½ tumblerful of broken Ice.

Half fill a tumbler with broken ice and add the
Angostura Bitters. Then add the Brown
Curaçao and the Gin. Stir well and pass
through a strainer into a cocktail glass. Serve
with a cherry and a dash of lemon peel juice
on top.

A cocktail of medium strength.

## GREAT GUNS COCKTAIL

*$\frac{1}{8}$ gill of French Vermouth*
*$\frac{1}{8}$ gill of Pale Sherry.*
*$\frac{1}{6}$ gill of Dubonnet.*
2 *dashes of Angostura Bitters.*
1 *dash of Lemon Peel Juice.*
1 *Cherry.*
$\frac{1}{2}$ *tumblerful of broken Ice.*

Half fill a tumbler with broken ice and add the French Vermouth. Then add the Dubonnet, the Sherry and the Angostura Bitters. Stir well and pass through a strainer into a cocktail glass. Serve with a cherry and a dash of lemon peel juice on top.

This cocktail can be varied by using Orange Bitters and orange peel juice instead of Angostura Bitters and lemon peel juice, respectively.

## HARRISON COCKTAIL

*$\frac{1}{3}$ gill of Gin.*
*$\frac{1}{6}$ gill of Lemon (or Lime), Juice.*
1 *teaspoonful of Angostura Bitters.*
$\frac{1}{2}$ *teaspoonful of powdered Sugar.*
$\frac{1}{2}$ *shakerful of broken Ice.*

The shaker is half filled with broken ice and the Gin is added. Then put in the powdered sugar, the lemon (or lime) juice and the Angostura Bitters. Shake well and pass through a strainer into a cocktail glass.

A medium strength cocktail, useful for serving at grown-up parties.

## HARVARD COCKTAIL

⅛ *gill of Italian Vermouth.*
⅛ *gill of Brandy.*
2 or 3 *dashes of Angostura Bitters.*
½ *teaspoonful of Plain Syrup.*
1 or 2 *dashes of Lemon Peel Juice.*
1 *Cherry.*
½ *tumblerful of broken Ice.*

Half fill the tumbler with broken ice and add the Angostura Bitters. Then add the Italian Vermouth, the Plain Syrup and the Brandy. Stir up and pass through a strainer into a cocktail glass. Serve with a cherry and a dash of lemon peel juice on top.

This cocktail is fairly strong.

## HOLLYWOOD COCKTAIL

⅛ *gill of French Vermouth.*
⅛ *gill of Italian Vermouth.*
¼ *gill of Dry Gin.*
2 *dashes of Brown Curaçao.*
1 *dash of Lemon Peel Juice.*
1 *Cherry.*
½ *tumblerful of broken Ice.*

Half fill the tumbler with broken ice and add the French Vermouth. Then put in the Italian Vermouth, the Dry Gin and the Brown Curaçao. Stir well and pass through a strainer

into a cocktail glass. Serve with a cherry
and a dash of lemon peel juice on top.

This cocktail is very popular in America.

If required dry, double the quantity of
French Vermouth and leave out the Italian.

### IKA COCKTAIL

$\frac{1}{6}$ *gill of Grenadine Syrup.*
$\frac{1}{3}$ *gill of Gin.*
1 *dash of Lemon Peel Juice.*
$\frac{1}{2}$ *tumblerful of broken Ice.*

The tumbler is half filled with broken ice and
the Grenadine Syrup is added. Now add the
Gin and stir well. Strain into a cocktail glass
and serve with a dash of lemon peel juice on
top.

A very pleasant cocktail of medium strength

### INCA COCKTAIL

$\frac{1}{8}$ *gill of Gin.*
$\frac{1}{8}$ *gill of French Vermouth.*
$\frac{1}{8}$ *gill of Dry Sherry.*
1 *teaspoonful of Orange Bitters.*
1 *teaspoonful of Plain Syrup.*
1 *dash of Orange Peel Juice.*
1 *Cherry.*
$\frac{1}{2}$ *tumblerful of broken Ice.*

The tumbler is half filled with broken ice and
the Orange Bitters is added. Next add the
Gin, the French Vermouth, the Pale Sherry
and the Plain Syrup. Stir well and pass

through a strainer into a cocktail glass. Serve with a cherry and a dash of orange peel juice on top.

## INDIAN COCKTAIL

⅛ *gill of Canadian Club Whisky.*
⅛ *gill of Italian Vermouth.*
⅛ *gill of Gin.*
½ *teaspoonful of Triple Sec Cointreau.*
½ *teaspoonful of Orange Bitters.*
½ *teaspoonful of Brown Curaçao.*
1 *dash of Lemon Peel Juice.*
½ *tumblerful of broken Ice.*

Half fill a tumbler with broken ice and add the Orange Bitters. Then add the Canadian Club Whisky, the Italian Vermouth, the Gin, the Cointreau and the Brown Curaçao. Stir well and pass through a strainer into a cocktail glass. Serve with a dash of lemon peel juice on top.

This is a fairly strong cocktail, not advised in hot weather.

## JACK ROSE COCKTAIL

1 *teaspoonful of Grenadine Syrup.*
⅓ *gill of Calvados.*
⅙ *gill of Lemon Juice.*
1 *or 2 dashes of Lemon Peel Juice.*
½ *shakerful of broken Ice.*

The shaker is half filled with broken ice and the lemon juice is added. Then add the Grenadine

Syrup and the Calvados.    Shake well and pass
through a strainer into a cocktail glass.    Serve
with a dash of lemon peel juice on top.

Lime juice may be substituted if desired.
This makes a pleasant change.

### J. J. MURPHY COCKTAIL
    ¼ *gill of Gin.*
    ⅛ *gill of French Vermouth.*
    ⅛ *gill of Italian Vermouth.*
    1 *dash of Bénédictine.*
    1 *dash of Lemon Peel Juice.*
    1 *Cherry.*
    ½ *tumblerful of broken Ice.*

Half fill the tumbler with broken ice and add
the Gin.    Now add the French Vermouth, the
Italian Vermouth and the Bénédictine.    Stir
well and pass through a strainer into a cocktail
glass.    Serve with a cherry and a dash of lemon
peel juice.    A cocktail of medium strength.

### KURSAAL COCKTAIL
    1 *dash of Angostura Bitters.*
    1 *dash of Orange Bitters.*
    ¼ *gill of Brandy.*
    ⅛ *gill of Cherry Brandy.*
    ⅛ *gill of French Vermouth.*
    1 *dash of Absinthe.*
    1 *teaspoonful of Plain Syrup.*
    1 *dash of Lemon Peel Juice.*
    1 *Cherry.*
    ½ *shakerful of broken Ice.*

Half fill the shaker with broken ice and add the Angostura Bitters. Then add the Orange Bitters, the Brandy, the Cherry Brandy, the French Vermouth, the Absinthe and the Plain Syrup. Shake well and pass through a strainer into a small wine glass. Serve with a cherry and a dash of lemon peel juice on top.

If you have no Cherry Brandy you can still make this cocktail by doubling the quantity of French Vermouth.

### LIDO COCKTAIL

½ *gill of Dry Gin.*
½ *gill of French Vermouth.*
2 *dashes of Apricot Brandy.*
1 *Cherry.*
½ *tumblerful of broken Ice.*

Half fill the tumbler with broken ice and add the Gin. Then add the French Vermouth and the Apricot Brandy. Stir well and pass through a strainer into a cocktail glass. Serve with a cherry.

If you have no Apricot Brandy you can use Cherry Brandy instead.

### LONDON COCKTAIL.

⅓ *gill of Dry Gin.*
1 *teaspoonful of Absinthe.*
1 *teaspoonful of Orange Bitters.*
2 *teaspoonfuls of Plain Syrup.*
1 *dash of Orange Peel Juice.*
½ *tumblerful of broken Ice.*

Half fill a tumbler with broken ice and add the Orange Bitters. Then add the Dry Gin, the Absinthe and the Plain Syrup. Stir well and pass through a strainer into a cocktail glass. Serve with a dash of orange peel juice on top.

If this is sweeter than desired, reduce the quantity of Plain Syrup.

## LUIGI COCKTAIL

*A few drops of Cointreau.*
*¼ gill of French Vermouth.*
*¼ gill of Gin.*
*2 or 3 dashes of Grenadine.*
*The juice of ½ an Orange.*
*1 dash of Orange Peel Juice.*
*½ shakerful of broken Ice.*

Half fill the shaker with broken ice and add the French Vermouth. Then add the Cointreau, the Gin, the Orange juice and the Grenadine. Shake well and pass through a strainer into a cocktail glass. Serve with a dash of orange peel juice on top.

Some people prefer to use tangerine juice and tangerine peel juice in place of the orange juice and the orange peel juice respectively. This makes a pleasant alternative.

## MALIBU COCKTAIL

$\frac{1}{3}$ gill of Gin.
$\frac{1}{6}$ gill of French Vermouth.
1 teaspoonful of Angostura Bitters.
1 teaspoonful of Absinthe.
1 Olive.
1 dash of Lemon Peel Juice.
$\frac{1}{2}$ tumblerful of broken Ice.

Half fill the tumbler with broken ice and add the Angostura Bitters. Then add the French Vermouth, the Gin and the Absinthe. Stir well and pass through a strainer into a cocktail glass. Serve with a dash of lemon peel juice on top.

This cocktail is named after the famous coast resort near Hollywood. It is very refreshing in hot weather.

## MANHATTAN COCKTAIL—1

$\frac{1}{4}$ gill of Canadian Club Whisky.
$\frac{1}{4}$ gill of Italian Vermouth.
1 or 2 dashes of Angostura Bitters.
1 Cherry.
$\frac{1}{2}$ tumblerful of broken Ice.

Half fill a tumbler with broken ice and first add the Canadian Club Whisky, then the Italian Vermouth and the Angostura Bitters. Stir well and pass through a strainer into a cocktail glass. Serve with a cherry.

One of the best-known cocktails : it deserves to be a favourite.

### MANHATTAN COCKTAIL—2 (Dry)

¼ *gill of Canadian Club Whisky.*
¼ *gill of French Vermouth.*
1 *or 2 dashes of Angostura Bitters.*
1 *Cherry.*
½ *tumblerful of broken Ice.*

This cocktail is prepared as in the previous case, but French Vermouth is used instead of Italian Vermouth. A much drier cocktail is the result.

### MANHATTAN COCKTAIL—3 (Medium)

¼ *gill of Canadian Club Whisky.*
⅛ *gill of Italian Vermouth.*
⅛ *gill of French Vermouth.*
1 *or 2 dashes of Angostura Bitters.*
1 *Cherry.*
½ *tumblerful of broken Ice.*

Make up as before, but in this case a blend of both Italian Vermouth and French Vermouth is used.

### MANHATTAN COCKTAIL—4

¼ *gill of Canadian Club Whisky.*
¼ *gill of Italian Vermouth.*
1 *dash of Angostura Bitters.*
1 *dash of Absinthe.*
2 *dashes of Brown Curaçao.*
1 *small piece of Orange or Lemon Peel.*
1 *Cherry.*
½ *tumblerful of broken Ice.*

Make up as before and serve with a piece of orange or lemon peel on top. This cocktail has a good deal more " kick " in it than the other Manhattans.

MARTINEZ COCKTAIL—1 (Sweet)

> ½ *gill of Italian Vermouth.*
> ¼ *gill of Gin.*
> 1 *or* 2 *dashes of Angostura Bitters.*
> 1 *dash of Lemon Peel Juice.*
> 1 *Cherry or Olive.*
> ½ *tumblerful of broken Ice.*

Half fill a tumbler with broken ice and add the Angostura Bitters. Then add the Italian Vermouth and the Gin. Stir well and pass through a strainer into a cocktail glass. Serve with a cherry or an olive and a dash of lemon peel juice on top. This cocktail is very popular.

MARTINEZ COCKTAIL—2 (Medium)

> ⅛ *gill of French Vermouth.*
> ⅛ *gill of Italian Vermouth.*
> ¼ *gill of Gin.*
> 1 *or* 2 *dashes of Angostura Bitters.*
> 1 *dash of Lemon Peel Juice.*
> 1 *Cherry or Olive.*
> ½ *tumblerful of broken Ice.*

This cocktail is made up in exactly the same way as the previous one except that both French Vermouth and Italian Vermouth are used instead of only Italian.

## MARTINEZ COCKTAIL—3 (Dry)

¼ *gill of French Vermouth.*
¼ *gill of Gin.*
1 *or* 2 *dashes of Angostura Bitters.*
1 *dash of Lemon Peel Juice.*
1 *Cherry or Olive.*
½ *tumblerful of broken Ice.*

This cocktail is made up in exactly the same way as the Sweet Martini cocktail; but French Vermouth is used instead of Italian Vermouth.

## MARTINEZ SPECIAL COCKTAIL

⅛ *gill of French Vermouth.*
¼ *gill of Gin.*
1½ *teaspoonfuls of Maraschino.*
1 *teaspoonful of Orange Bitters.*
½ *teaspoonful of Angostura Bitters.*
1 *dash of Orange Peel Juice.*
1 *Cherry or Olive.*
½ *shakerful of broken Ice.*

This cocktail is made up in exactly the same way as the previous cocktail except that the Maraschino and the Orange Bitters are added, and also, that it is served with a dash of orange peel juice instead of lemon.

## MARTINI COCKTAIL—1
### (Sweet)

$\frac{1}{3}$ *gill of Dry Gin.*
$\frac{1}{6}$ *gill of Italian Vermouth (Martini's).*
$\frac{1}{2}$ *teaspoonful of Orange Bitters.*
1 *or* 2 *dashes of Lemon Peel Juice.*
$\frac{1}{2}$ *tumblerful of broken Ice.*

Half fill the tumbler with broken ice and add the Dry Gin. Then add the Italian Vermouth and the Orange Bitters. Stir well and pass through a strainer into a cocktail glass. Squeeze 1 or 2 dashes of lemon peel juice on top.

This is the original recipe and it has never been improved upon.

## MARTINI COCKTAIL—2
### (Medium)

$\frac{1}{8}$ *gill of French Vermouth.*
$\frac{1}{8}$ *gill of Italian Vermouth.*
$\frac{1}{4}$ *gill of Dry Gin.*
$\frac{1}{2}$ *tumblerful of broken Ice.*
1 *or* 2 *dashes of Lemon Peel Juice.*

Make up as before, but in this case a blend of both Italian Vermouth and French Vermouth is used.

## MARTINI COCKTAIL—3
### (Dry)

$\frac{1}{4}$ *gill of Dry Gin.*
$\frac{1}{4}$ *gill of French Vermouth.*
1 *dash of Lemon Peel Juice.*
$\frac{1}{2}$ *tumblerful of broken Ice.*

Make up in exactly the same way as the Sweet Martini Cocktail; but use French Vermouth instead of Italian Vermouth.


## MARTINI SPECIAL COCKTAIL

$\frac{1}{4}$ *gill of Dry Gin.*
$\frac{1}{8}$ *gill of Italian Vermouth.*
1 *teaspoonful of Raspberry Syrup.*
$\frac{1}{2}$ *teaspoonful of Absinthe.*
$\frac{1}{2}$ *teaspoonful of Maraschino.*
1 *dash of Lemon Peel Juice.*
$\frac{1}{2}$ *shakerful of broken Ice.*

The shaker is half filled with broken ice and the Raspberry Syrup is added. Then add the Italian Vermouth, the Dry Gin, the Absinthe and the Maraschino. Shake up and pass through a strainer into a cocktail glass. Serve with a dash of lemon peel juice.

This makes a pleasant variation from the ordinary Martini cocktails.

## MIAMI COCKTAIL

¼ *gill of Pale Sherry.*
¼ *gill of Dubonnet.*
1 *teaspoonful of Orange Bitters.*
1 *dash of Orange Peel Juice.*
1 *Cherry.*
½ *tumblerful of broken Ice.*

Half fill a tumbler with broken ice and add the
Pale Sherry. Then put in the Orange Bitters
and the Dubonnet. Stir up and pass through a
strainer into a cocktail glass. Serve with a
cherry and a dash of orange peel juice on top.

A very refreshing cocktail.

## MILLIONAIRE COCKTAIL

1 *dash of Absinthe.*
⅛ *gill of Canadian Club Whisky.*
1 *teaspoonful of Grenadine Syrup.*
1 *teaspoonful of Brown Curaçao.*
1 *dash of Orange Bitters.*
*The white of a fresh Egg.*
½ *shakerful of broken Ice.*

Half fill the shaker with broken ice and add the
Orange Bitters. Then put in the Canadian
Club Whisky, the Brown Curaçao, the Absinthe
and the Grenadine Syrup. Shake well and
pass through a strainer into a cocktail glass.
Serve with a cherry.

The Absinthe improves the flavour of this
cocktail, but it can be omitted if desired.

C

## MONKEY GLAND COCKTAIL

⅛ *gill of Gin.*
⅛ *gill of Orange Juice.*
4 or 5 *dashes of Absinthe.*
6 or 7 *dashes of Grenadine Syrup.*
1 *dash of Orange Peel Juice.*
½ *shakerful of broken Ice.*

The shaker is half filled with broken ice and the Grenadine added. Then add the Absinthe, the Gin and the Orange juice. Shake well and pass through a strainer into a wine glass. Serve with a dash of orange peel juice on top.

Raspberry Syrup may be used instead of Grenadine Syrup, if desired. Both are rather sweet and some may prefer to reduce the quantity of the Syrup.

## MONTSERRAT COCKTAIL

⅓ *gill of Dry Gin.*
2 *dashes of Absinthe.*
1 *teaspoonful of Grenadine Syrup.*
2 *teaspoonfuls of Lime Juice.*
1 *Cherry.*
½ *shakerful of broken Ice.*

Half fill the shaker with broken ice and add the Dry Gin. Then add the Lime juice, the Grenadine Syrup and the Absinthe. Shake well and pass through a strainer into a cocktail glass. Serve with a cherry.

This cocktail is very refreshing and is of medium strength.

## MORNING COCKTAIL

⅓ *gill of Italian Vermouth.*
⅓ *gill of Brandy.*
1 *teaspoonful of Angostura Bitters.*
1 *teaspoonful of Absinthe.*
1 *teaspoonful of Maraschino.*
1 *Cherry.*
1 *slice of Lemon.*
½ *tumblerful of broken Ice.*

Half fill the tumbler with broken ice and add the Angostura Bitters. Then put in the Absinthe, the Brandy, the Italian Vermouth and the Maraschino. Stir well and strain into a wine glass. Serve with a cherry and a slice of lemon.

This recipe can be varied by reducing, by half, the quantity of Maraschino and by adding ½ teaspoonful of Brown Curaçao.

## MURMURER COCKTAIL

¼ *gill of Gin.*
¼ *gill of Sherry.*
⅛ *teaspoonful of Angostura Bitters.*
¼ *teaspoonful of Lime Juice.*
1 *dash of Lemon Peel Juice.*
½ *tumblerful of broken Ice.*

Half fill the tumbler with broken ice and add the Angostura Bitters. Then add the Gin, the Sherry and the Lime juice. Stir well and pass through a strainer into a cocktail glass. Serve with a dash of lemon peel juice on top.

This is a very pleasant cocktail of medium strength.

### OLD-FASHIONED COCKTAIL

    1 *lump of Loaf Sugar.*
    1 *teaspoonful of Orange Bitters.*
    1 *teaspoonful of Angostura Bitters.*
    ½ *gill of Bénédictine.*
    1 *dash of Lemon Peel Juice.*
    1½ *tablespoonfuls of Water.*
    1 *small lump of Ice.*

This cocktail is prepared and served in a large wine glass. Put the lump of sugar in the wine glass and add the water. Then crush the sugar with a spoon and add the lump of ice, the Orange Bitters, the Angostura Bitters and the Bénédictine. Stir well and serve with a dash of lemon peel juice on top.

Any other Liqueur can be used in place of the Bénédictine, if desired.

### OLIVETTE COCKTAIL

    ¼ *gill of French Vermouth.*
    ¼ *gill of Dry Gin.*
    2 *dashes of Plain Syrup.*
    2 *dashes of Absinthe.*
    2 *dashes of Angostura Bitters.*
    2 *dashes of Orange Bitters.*
    2 *dashes of Lemon Peel Juice.*
    1 *Olive.*
    ⅓ *tumblerful of broken Ice.*

Half fill a tumbler with broken ice and add the
Orange Bitters. Then add the Angostura
Bitters, the Plain Syrup, the French Vermouth,
the Dry Gin and the Absinthe. Stir well and
pass through a strainer into a small wine glass.
Serve with an olive and a dash of lemon peel
juice on top.

If preferred, Italian Vermouth can be used
instead of French.

### ORANGE BLOSSOM COCKTAIL

*¼ gill of Dry Gin.*
*¼ gill of Orange Squash.*
*½ teaspoonful of Grenadine Syrup.*
*A few drops of Orange Bitters.*
*1 dash of Orange Peel Juice.*
*½ shakerful of broken Ice.*

Half fill the shaker with broken ice and add the
Orange Bitters. Then add the Dry Gin, the
Grenadine Syrup and the Orange Squash.
Shake well and strain into a cocktail glass.
Serve with a dash of orange peel juice on top.

If this is sweeter than required, reduce the
quantity of Grenadine Syrup.

### PARADISE COCKTAIL

*⅛ gill of Gin.*
*⅛ gill of Lemon Squash.*
*¼ gill of Apricot Brandy.*
*1 slice of Lemon.*
*1 dash of Lemon Peel Juice.*
*½ shakerful of broken Ice.*

Half fill the shaker with broken ice and add the
Dry Gin. Then add the Lemon Squash and
the Apricot Brandy. Shake well and pass
through a strainer into a cocktail glass. Serve
with a dash of lemon peel juice on top.

This recipe can be varied by using Orange
juice, Tangerine juice, or Grape-fruit juice
instead of Lemon Squash. All are excellent.

### PERFECT COCKTAIL

$\frac{1}{6}$ *gill of Italian Vermouth.*
$\frac{1}{6}$ *gill of French Vermouth.*
$\frac{1}{2}$ *gill of Dry Gin.*
2 *dashes of Absinthe.*
1 *dash of Lemon Peel Juice.*
1 *slice of Lemon.*
$\frac{1}{2}$ *shakerful of broken Ice.*

Half fill the shaker with broken ice and add the
Italian Vermouth. Then put in the French
Vermouth, the Dry Gin and the Absinthe.
Shake well and pass through a strainer into a
wine glass. Serve with a slice of lemon and a
dash of lemon peel juice on top.

This cocktail is pleasant and fairly strong.

### PING PONG COCKTAIL

$\frac{1}{4}$ *gill of Sloe Gin.*
$\frac{1}{4}$ *gill of Italian Vermouth.*
1 *dash of Angostura Bitters.*
1 *Cherry.*
$\frac{1}{2}$ *tumblerful of broken Ice.*

Half fill the tumbler with broken ice and add the Angostura Bitters. Then add the Sloe Gin and the Italian Vermouth. Stir well and pass through a strainer into a cocktail glass. Serve with a cherry.

Another way of making up this cocktail is to use French Vermouth in place of Italian.

### PLAZA COCKTAIL

¼ *gill of Dry Gin.*
⅛ *gill of French Vermouth.*
⅛ *gill of Italian Vermouth.*
1 *small slice of Pineapple.*
½ *shakerful of broken Ice.*

Half fill the shaker with the ice and add the Dry Gin. Then add the French Vermouth and the Italian Vermouth. Shake well and strain into a cocktail glass. Serve with a slice of pineapple on top.

### RIALTO COCKTAIL

2 *dashes of Orange Bitters.*
½ *gill of Calvados.*
¼ *gill of Italian Vermouth.*
1 *dash of Orange Squash.*
1 *slice of Orange.*
2 *springs of Mint.*
2 *lumps of Sugar.*
½ *tumblerful of broken Ice.*

Half fill a tumbler with broken ice and add 1 sprig of mint. Then, add the sugar, the

Orange Bitters, the Italian Vermouth, the Orange squash and the Calvados. Stir well and pass through a strainer into a cocktail glass. Serve with a slice of orange and a sprig of mint. This is a delightful cocktail, fairly strong.

## RIVIERA COCKTAIL

½ *gill of Dry Gin.*
¼ *gill of Calvados.*
3 *or* 4 *dashes of Lemon Squash.*
1 *dash of Grenadine Syrup.*
1 *slice of Lemon.*
½ *shakerful of broken Ice.*

The shaker is half filled with broken ice and the Lemon Squash is added. Then add the Grenadine Syrup, the Dry Gin and the Calvados. Shake well and pass through a strainer into a small wine glass. Serve with a slice of lemon. This cocktail is very popular in Paris and on the Riviera.

## ROB ROY COCKTAIL

⅛ *gill of Scotch Whisky.*
⅛ *gill of French Vermouth.*
2 *dashes of Angostura Bitters.*
1 *dash of Orange Bitters.*
2 *dashes of Brown Curaçao.*
2 *dashes of Lemon Peel Juice.*
1 *Cherry.*
⅛ *tumblerful of broken Ice.*

Half fill the tumbler with broken ice and add the Orange Bitters. Then add the Angostura Bitters, the French Vermouh, the Scotch Whisky and the Curaçao. Stir well and pass through a strainer into a cocktail glass. Serve with a cherry and a dash of lemon peel juice on top.

The Curaçao can be omitted, if desired. Another variation is to use Italian Vermouth in place of French.

### ROSE COCKTAIL

⅙ *gill of French Vermouth.*
⅙ *gill of Dry Gin.*
⅙ *gill of Orange Juice.*
1 *teaspoonful of Grenadine Syrup.*
1 *dash of Orange Peel Juice.*
½ *shakerful of broken Ice.*

Half fill the shaker with broken ice and add the French Vermouth. Then, add the Grenadine Syrup, the Orange juice and the Dry Gin Shake well and pass through a strainer into a cocktail glass. Serve with a cherry and a dash of orange peel juice on top.

Some people prefer to add a dash of Dubonnet. This improves the cocktail, in the opinions of some connoisseurs.

### ROYAL CLOVER CLUB COCKTAIL

½ *gill of Dry Gin.*
1 *teaspoonful of Grenadine Syrup.*
*The juice of a Lemon.*
*The yolk of an Egg.*
1 *dash of Nutmeg.*
½ *shakerful of broken Ice.*

This cocktail is prepared in exactly the same
way as the Clover Club Cocktail—1, except
that the yolk is used instead of the white of
an egg.

If preferred, half the quantity of Dry Gin
may be used and ⅛ gill of French Vermouth
added.

### ROYAL COCKTAIL

¼ *gill of Dubonnet.*
½ *gill of Gin.*
2 *dashes of Orange Bitters.*
1 *or 2 dashes of Orange Peel Juice.*
1 *Cherry.*
½ *tumblerful of broken Ice.*

The tumbler is half filled with broken ice and
the Orange Bitters added. Then, add the
Dubonnet and the Gin. Stir well and pass
through a strainer into a small wine glass.
Serve with a cherry and a dash of orange peel
juice on top.

This cocktail makes an excellent *apéritif.*

# How To Mix Them

## RUM COCKTAIL

⅛ *gill of Rum.*
2 *dashes of Angostura Bitters.*
1 *dash of Brown Curaçao.*
1 *dash of Lemon Peel Juice.*
1 *Cherry.*
½ *tumblerful of broken Ice.*

This cocktail is made up in exactly the same way as the Gin cocktail, but Rum is used instead of Gin.

## SHANGHAI COCKTAIL

⅛ *gill of Brandy.*
1 *teaspoonful of Brown Curaçao.*
1 *teaspoonful of Plain Syrup.*
1 *teaspoonful of Maraschino.*
1 *teaspoonful of Angostura Bitters.*
1 *dash of Lemon Peel juice.*
1 *Cherry.*
½ *tumblerful of broken Ice.*

Half fill the tumbler with broken ice and add the Angostura Bitters. Then add the Plain Syrup, the Maraschino, the Brown Curaçao and the Brandy. Stir well and pass through a strainer into a cocktail glass. Serve with a cherry and a dash of lemon peel juice on top.

Some people prefer to omit the Maraschino.

## SHERRY COCKTAIL

⅛ *gill of Sherry.*
2 *dashes of Angostura Bitters.*
2 *dashes of Orange Bitters.*
1 *dash of Orange Peel Juice.*
1 *Cherry.*
½ *tumblerful of broken Ice.*

This cocktail is made up in exactly the same
way as the Gin cocktail except that Sherry and
Orange Bitters are used instead of Gin and
Brown Curaçao.

## SIDECAR COCKTAIL—1

¼ *gill of Brandy.*
⅛ *gill of Dry Gin.*
*The juice of ¼ Lemon.*
½ *shakerful of broken Ice.*

Half fill the shaker with broken ice and squeeze
in the juice of ¼ lemon. Then add the Brandy
and the Dry Gin. Shake well and pass
through a strainer into a cocktail glass.

This is a great favourite among the French
and is fairly strong.

## SIDECAR COCKTAIL—2

¼ *gill of Brandy.*
⅛ *gill of Cointreau.*
*The juice of ¼ lemon.*
½ *shakerful of broken Ice.*

This cocktail is made up in exactly the same
way as the previous one except that Cointreau
is used instead of Dry Gin.

### SILVER COCKTAIL

1 *teaspoonful of Orange Bitters.*
1 *teaspoonful of Maraschino.*
$\frac{1}{6}$ *gill of Italian Vermouth.*
$\frac{1}{3}$ *gill of Dry Gin.*
1 *dash of Lemon Peel Juice.*
1 *Cherry.*
$\frac{1}{2}$ *shakerful of broken Ice.*

The shaker is half filled with broken ice and the
Orange Bitters added. Then add the Dry
Gin, the Italian Vermouth and the Maraschino.
Shake well and strain into a cocktail glass.
Serve with a cherry and a dash of lemon peel
juice on top. A cocktail of medium strength.

### STAR COCKTAIL

1 *teaspoonful of Brown Curaçao.*
2 *dashes of Orange Bitters.*
$\frac{1}{4}$ *gill of Calvados.*
$\frac{1}{4}$ *gill of Italian Vermouth.*
1 *dash of Lemon Peel Juice.*
1 *slice of Lemon.*
$\frac{1}{2}$ *tumblerful of broken Ice.*

Half fill the tumbler with broken ice and add
the Orange Bitters. Then add the Calvados,
the Italian Vermouth and the Brown Curaçao.
Stir well and pass through a strainer into a
cocktail glass. Serve with a slice of lemon and
a dash of lemon peel juice on top.

This cocktail is sometimes served with an
Olive in place of the slice of lemon.

### SUNSHINE COCKTAIL

¼ *gill of Gin.*
⅛ *gill of Italian Vermouth.*
¼ *gill of Orange Squash.*
1 *teaspoonful of Orange Bitters.*
1 *teaspoonful of Grenadine Syrup.*
1 *Cherry.*
½ *tumblerful of broken Ice.*

The tumbler is half filled with broken ice and
the Orange Bitters added. Then add the
Italian Vermouth, the Gin, the Orange
Squash and the Grenadine Syrup. Stir well
and pass through a strainer into a small wine
glass. Serve with a cherry.

A very pleasant cocktail of medium strength.

### TOP NOTCH COCKTAIL

1 *teaspoonful of Raspberry Syrup.*
¼ *gill of French Vermouth.*
¼ *gill of Sloe Gin.*
1 *Cherry.*
½ *shakerful of broken Ice.*

Half fill a shaker with broken ice. Then put
in the French Vermouth, the Sloe Gin and the
Raspberry Syrup. Stir well and pass through
a strainer into a cocktail glass. Serve with a
cherry. This is a sweet cocktail and is very
popular among the fair sex.

### TORONTO COCKTAIL

¼ *gill of Dry Gin.*
⅛ *gill of Scotch Whisky.*
⅛ *gill of Dubonnet.*

1 *dash of Lemon Peel Juice.*
1 *Cherry.*
½ *tumblerful of broken Ice.*

The tumbler is half filled with broken ice and the Dry Gin added. Then add the Scotch Whisky and the Dubonnet. Stir well and pass through a strainer into a cocktail glass. Serve with a cherry and a dash of lemon peel juice on top. An excellent *apéritif.*

## TURF COCKTAIL

1 *teaspoonful of Orange Bitters.*
⅓ *gill of Dry Gin.*
⅙ *gill of French Vermouth.*
1 *teaspoonful of Absinthe.*
1 *teaspoonful of Maraschino.*
1 *Olive.*
½ *tumblerful of broken Ice.*

Half fill a tumbler with broken ice and add the Orange Bitters. Then add the Dry Gin, the French Vermouth, the Absinthe and the Maraschino. Stir well and pass through a strainer into a cocktail glass. Serve with an olive.

This cocktail is very popular. If desired Peach Bitters can be used in place of Orange Bitters.

## TUXEDO COCKTAIL

1 *teaspoonful of Angostura Bitters.*
⅙ *gill of Italian Vermouth.*
⅛ *gill of Gin.*
2 *dashes of Absinthe.*

1 *teaspoonful of Maraschino.*
1 *dash of Lemon Peel Juice.*
1 *Cherry.*
½ *tumblerful of broken Ice.*

The tumbler is half filled with broken ice and the Angostura Bitters added.    Then add the Italian Vermouth, the Gin, the Maraschino and the Absinthe.   Stir well and pass through a strainer into a small wine glass.   Serve with a cherry and a dash of lemon peel juice on top.

This is a very popular cocktail.

### WHISKY COCKTAIL
⅓ *gill of Scotch Whisky.*
1 *dash of Angostura Bitters.*
2 *dashes of Brown Curaçao.*
1 *dash of Lemon Peel Juice.*
1 *Cherry.*
1 *lump of Sugar.*
½ *tumblerful of broken Ice.*

Make up in exactly the same way as for Gin cocktail, but use the altered ingredients.

### WONDER BAR COCKTAIL
⅓ *gill of Dry Gin.*
⅛ *gill of Italian Vermouth.*
⅛ *gill of French Vermouth.*
1 *dash of Absinthe.*
½ *teaspoonful of Angostura Bitters.*
½ *teaspoonful of Orange Bitters.*
1 *dash of Lemon Peel Juice.*
1 *Cherry.*
⅓ *tumblerful of broken Ice*

Half fill the tumbler with broken ice and add
the Angostura Bitters. Then add the Orange
Bitters, the Italian Vermouth, the French
Vermouth and the Dry Gin. Stir well and
pass through a strainer into a small wine
glass. Serve with a cherry and a dash of
lemon peel juice on top.

This is a pleasant and fairly strong cocktail.

### YOKOHAMA COCKTAIL
⅙ *gill of Gin.*
⅙ *gill of Italian Vermouth.*
⅙ *gill of Crème de Menthe.*
1 *dash of Lemon Peel Juice.*
1 *Olive.*
½ *shakerful of broken Ice.*

Half fill the shaker with broken ice and add the
Gin. Then add the Italian Vermouth and the
Crème de Menthe. Shake well and pass
through a strainer into a cocktail glass. Serve
with an olive and a dash of lemon peel juice
on top.

If required not quite so sweet, use French
Vermouth in place of Italian.

### YORK COCKTAIL
¼ *gill of Scotch Whisky.*
¼ *gill of Italian Vermouth.*
1 *dash of Orange Bitters.*
1 *dash of Angostura Bitters.*
1 *dash of Lemon Peel Juice.*
½ *shakerful of broken Ice.*

5—C

Half fill a tumbler with broken ice and add the
Orange Bitters. Then add the Angostura
Bitters, the Italian Vermouth and the Scotch
Whisky. Stir well and pass through a
strainer into a cocktail glass. Serve with a
dash of lemon peel juice on top.

If you prefer the dry type of cocktail, you
can use French Vermouth in place of Italian.

## ZA ZA COCKTAIL

½ *gill of Dubonnet.*
¼ *gill of Dry Gin.*
2 *dashes of Angostura Bitters.*
½ *shakerful of broken Ice.*

Half fill the shaker with broken ice and add
the Angostura Bitters. Then add the Dry
Gin and the Dubonnet. Shake well and pass
through a strainer into a cocktail glass.

This cocktail is an excellent *apéritif.*

## ZERO HOUR COCKTAIL

2 *dashes of Absinthe.*
3 *dashes of Crème de Menthe.*
¼ *gill of Brandy.*
⅛ *gill of Apricot Brandy.*
1 *Olive.*
½ *shakerful of broken Ice.*

The shaker is half filled with broken ice and
the Brandy added. Then the Apricot Brandy and
the Crème de Menthe are added. Shake well
and pass through a strainer into a cocktail
glass. Serve with an olive and two dashes of
Absinthe on top.

## SECTION II

# FRUIT COCKTAILS

*(Mostly Non-Alcoholic)*

### APRICOT COCKTAIL

*Apricots.*
*Pineapple Chunks.*
*1 tablespoonful of Cream.*
*1 teaspoonfuls of Lemon Juice.*
*2 teaspoonful of Apricot Syrup.*
*Ice Chips.*

Slice the Apricots and Pineapple chunks and put in a small bowl. Then add the lemon juice and the Apricot Syrup. Stand on ice chips until thoroughly cold. Serve with a tablespoonful of cream on top.

### BLACKCURRANT COCKTAIL

*½ Grape Fruit.*
*¼ cupful of Blackcurrants.*
*2 teaspoonfuls of powdered Sugar.*

Cut a hole in the middle of the half grape fruit and fill with blackcurrants. Serve with powdered sugar on top.

Any small fruit in season, such as Rasp-

berries, Gooseberries, Cherries, etc., may be
used in place of blackcurrants if desired.

## CHERRY COCKTAIL

1 *dash of Angostura Bitters.*
¼ *gill of Ginger Syrup.*
¼ *gill of Cherry Syrup.*
2 *dashes of Lime Juice.*
2 *slices of Orange.*
4 *or* 5 *stoned Cherries.*
1 *gill of Soda Water*
½ *tumblerful of broken Ice.*

Half fill the tumbler with broken ice and add
the Angostura Bitters. Then put in the
Ginger Syrup, the Cherry Syrup and the
Lime Juice. Stir well and pass through a
strainer into a tumbler. Fill up with Soda
Water. Serve with slices of orange and
cherries.

## CIDER COCKTAIL

1 *dash of Angostura Bitters.*
¾ *gill of Cider.*
½ *teaspoonful of Plain Syrup.*
1 *slice of Lemon.*
½ *tumblerful of broken Ice.*

Half fill the tumbler with broken ice and add
the Angostura Bitters. Then add the Plain
Syrup and the Cider. Stir well and pass
through a strainer into a small wine glass.
Serve with a slice of lemon on top.

Use non-alcoholic Cider if desired.

### GRAPE COCKTAIL

1 *dash of Angostura Bitters.*
¼ *gill of Grape Juice.*
½ *gill of Plain Syrup.*
2 *slices of fresh Fruit.*
1 *gill of Soda Water.*
½ *tumblerful of broken Ice.*

Half fill the tumbler with broken ice and add the Angostura Bitters. Then add the Grape juice and the Plain Syrup. Stir well and pass through a strainer into a tumbler. Fill up with Soda Water. Serve with slices of fresh fruit on top.

A delightful drink in hot weather, and one that contains a good deal of vitamin.

### GRAPE FRUIT COCKTAIL

1 *Grape Fruit.*
1 *small tin of Pineapple Chunks.*
1 *gill of Sherry.*
2 *Bananas.*
*Strawberries or Glacé Fruits.*
*Ice Chips.*

Remove the peel, pulp and pips from the Grape Fruit and press it through a sieve. Slice the bananas and pineapple thinly; add them to the grape fruit purée, in equal quantities, making 1 pint all together. Sprinkle castor sugar on the fruit and pour over it the Sherry. Stand on ice for about an hour.

Serve in sherbert glasses and decorate with fresh strawberries or glacé fruits.

## MINT COCKTAIL

1 *dash of Angostura Bitters.*
½ *gill of Crème de Menthe.*
⅓ *gill of Lime Juice.*
*Slices of fresh Fruit.*
2 *sprigs of Mint.*
¾ *gill of Soda Water.*
½ *tumblerful of broken Ice.*

Half fill a tumbler with broken ice and add the Angostura Bitters. Then add the Crème de Menthe and the Lime Juice. Stir well and pass through a strainer into a tumbler. Fill up with Soda Water. Serve with slices of fresh fruit on top.

If desired, you can alter the flavour of this cocktail by using Peppermint in place of Crème de Menthe.

## MIXED FRUIT COCKTAIL

1 *Orange.*
½ *Grape Fruit.*
1 *Banana.*
1 *cupful of Grapes with the seeds removed.*
7 or 8 *Cherries.*
3 *dashes of Maraschino (or Pineapple Syrup).*
2 *teaspoonfuls of powdered Sugar.*

Peel the orange and the half of a grape fruit, separate into sections and put into a large sundae glass. Then add the banana (cut in slices), the grapes and the cherries. Pour over the top 3 dashes of Maraschino or Pineapple Syrup and sprinkle with powdered sugar.

## ORANGES AND LEMONS COCKTAIL

    1 *Orange.*
    1 *Lemon.*
    2 or 3 *Cherries.*
    1 *dash of Peppermint.*
    2 *teaspoonfuls of powdered Sugar.*

Peel the orange and lemon, separate into sections and place in a sundae glass. Put the cherries in the centre of the glass and add the dash of Peppermint. Serve with the powdered sugar on top.

This recipe is very popular because it can be prepared so easily with ingredients that are present in every household.

## RASPBERRY SMASH COCKTAIL

    1 *dash of Angostura Bitters.*
    $\frac{1}{4}$ *gill of Raspberry Juice and Pulp.*
    $\frac{1}{4}$ *gill of Lemon Juice.*
    *A few Raspberries.*
    1$\frac{1}{4}$ *gills of Soda Water.*
    $\frac{1}{2}$ *tumblerful of broken Ice.*

This fruit cocktail is prepared in exactly the same way as Grape cocktail except that Raspberry juice and pulp is used in place of Grape juice. Serve with a few cherries on

top instead of slices of lemon and fresh fruit.
If preferred, Loganberries or Blackberries
may be used in place of Raspberries.

### REFRESHER COCKTAIL
> *Strawberries.*
> *Lemon Juice.*
> *Water.*
> ½ *shakerful of broken Ice.*

Take a small quantity of strawberries, currants,
raspberries or similar fruit in season. Squeeze
out the juice and strain into a shaker half
full of broken ice. Pour in half as much
lemon juice as fruit juice and add a little water.
Shake well and strain into a tumbler.

### SUN DEW COCKTAIL
> 1 *dash of Angostura Bitters.*
> ¼ *gill of Plain Syrup.*
> ¼ *gill of Grape Juice.*
> ½ *gill of Orange Juice.*
> 2 *slices of Orange.*
> ¾ *gill of Soda Water.*
> ½ *tumblerful of broken Ice.*

Half fill the tumbler with broken ice and add
the Angostura Bitters. Then put in the
Orange juice, the Plain Syrup and the Grape
juice. Stir well and pass through a strainer
into a tumbler. Fill up with Soda Water.
Serve with slices of orange on top.

A delightful drink—very refreshing.

# SECTION III

# MISCELLANEOUS DRINKS

*(These are not true Cocktails : but very much like them)*

### ABSINTHE COOLER

½ *gill of Whisky.*
2 *or 3 dashes of Absinthe.*
⅛ *gill of Lemon Juice.*
2 *dashes of Angostura Bitters.*
½ *pint of Ginger Ale.*
1 *lump of Ice.*

Put the lump of ice in a tall glass and add the Angostura Bitters. Then add the Whisky, the Lemon juice and the Ginger Ale. Stir well. Serve with two or three dashes of Absinthe on top.

A pleasant drink.

### ANGEL'S KISS

¼ *gill of Cream.*
¼ *gill of Bénédictine.*

Use a cocktail glass. Put the Bénédictine

into the cocktail glass. Then put in the
cream ; do not stir. A very popular drink.

## ANGOSTURA FIZZ

¼ *gill of Angostura Bitters.*
½ *gill of Lemon Juice.*
⅛ *gill of Plain Syrup.*
*The white of an Egg.*
*Soda Water.*
½ *shakerful of broken Ice.*

Half fill the shaker with broken ice and add the
Plain Syrup. Then add the Angostura Bitters,
the Lemon juice and the white of an egg.
Shake well and pass through a strainer into a
tumbler. To serve, fill up with Soda Water.

## BACARDI CRUSTA

⅓ *gill of Bacardi.*
⅙ *gill of Lemon Juice.*
1 *teaspoonful of Plain Syrup.*
1 *teaspoonful of Absinthe.*
2 *dashes of Angostura Bitters.*
*The peel of a Lemon cut in a spiral.*
*Slices of fresh Fruit.*
½ *teaspoonful of powdered Sugar.*
½ *shakerful of broken Ice.*

This drink is prepared in exactly the same way
as the Brandy Crusta except that Bacardi is
used in place of Brandy. Also the Orange
Bitters is left out and double the quantity of
Angostura Bitters is used.

Some people prefer to use Maraschino in place of Absinthe.

## BADMINTON CUP

1 *bottle of Claret.*
2 *bottles of Soda Water.*
*The juice and rind of* 1 *Lemon.*
3 *slices of Cucumber.*
3 *ozs. of Icing Sugar.*
¾ *gill of Brown Curaçao.*
*Ice Chips.*

Put the Claret into a large bowl and add the sugar. Then add the Lemon juice and the Brown Curaçao. Stir well. Surround the bowl with the ice and leave for half an hour; then strain the mixture and add the Soda water. Serve in a large tumbler with the lemon rind and the slices of cucumber on top.

## BRANDY COBBLER

1 *gill of Brandy.*
¼ *gill of Brown Curaçao.*
1 *dash of Lemon Peel Juice.*
2 *slices of Lemon.*
½ *tumblerful of broken Ice.*
½ *shakerful of broken Ice.*

This is prepared in exactly the same way as Whisky Cobbler. Use Brandy instead of Whisky.

A very refreshing drink.

## BRANDY CRUSTA

½ gill of Brandy.
⅙ gill of Lemon Juice.
1 teaspoonful of Plain Syrup.
1 teaspoonful of Maraschino.
1 dash of Orange Bitters.
1 dash of Angostura Bitters.
The peel of a Lemon cut in a spiral.
Slices of fresh Fruit.
½ teaspoonful of powdered Sugar.
½ shakerful of broken Ice.

Half fill the shaker with broken ice and add the
Orange Bitters.    Then add the Angostura
Bitters, the Lemon juice, the Plain Syrup, the
Brandy and the Maraschino.   Shake well and
strain.   Now moisten the inside of a wine
glass with Lemon juice and sprinkle with
sugar.   Then put in the lemon peel, cut spiral
fashion, and add the mixture.  Serve with
slices of fruit.

## BRANDY DAISY

½ gill of Brandy.
¼ gill of Lime Juice.
¼ gill of Lemon Juice.
¼ gill of Grenadine Syrup.
Slices of fresh Fruit.
Soda Water.
½ shakerful of broken Ice.

Half fill the shaker with broken ice and add the
Brandy.   Then put in the Lime juice, the

Lemon juice, and the Grenadine Syrup.
Shake well, pass through a strainer into a
large tumbler and fill up with Soda Water.
Serve with slices of fresh fruit on top and with a
spoon.

If you prefer it, you can halve the quantities
of the above ingredients and serve in a large
wine glass without adding the Soda Water.

## BRANDY EGG NOGG

½ *gill of Rum.*
½ *gill of Brandy.*
1 *teaspoonful of Sugar.*
1 *Egg.*
1 *dash of grated Nutmeg.*
¾ *gill of Milk.*
½ *shakerful of broken Ice.*

Prepare in exactly the same way as for Egg
Nogg.

This recipe is much stronger than the Egg
Nogg recipe, owing to the larger quantity of
Rum used.

## BRANDY FIZZ

½ *gill of Brandy.*
¾ *gill of Lemon Juice.*
⅙ *gill of Grenadine Syrup.*
1 *teaspoonful of Brown Curaçao.*
*The white of an Egg.*
*Soda Water.*
½ *shakerful of broken Ice.*

Half fill the shaker with broken ice and add the Lemon juice. Then add the Grenadine Syrup, the white of an egg, the Brandy and the Brown Curaçao. Shake well and pass through a strainer into a tumbler. To serve, fill up the tumbler with Soda Water.

This drink is very pleasant and a very good pick-me-up.

## BULLDOG COOLER

½ *gill of Dry Gin.*
1 *or* 2 *dashes of Orange Peel Juice.*
*The juice of half an Orange.*
1 *or* 2 *dashes of Plain Syrup.*
⅓ *pint of Ginger Ale.*
1 *lump of Ice.*

Put the lump of ice in a tall glass. Then add the Dry Gin, the Orange juice, the Plain syrup and the Ginger Ale. Stir well and serve with a dash of orange peel juice on top.

If this is sweeter than required, reduce the quantity of Plain Syrup.

## BURGUNDY CUP

1 *bottle of Burgundy.*
½ *gill of Brandy.*
½ *gill of Maraschino.*
¼ *gill of Brown Curaçao.*
2 *or* 3 *dashes of Bénédictine.*
2 *or* 3 *slices of Lemon.*
1 *or* 2 *slices of Orange.*

*Slices of fresh Fruit.*
1 *bottle of Soda Water.*
1 *big lump of Ice.*

Put the piece of ice into a large bowl and add the Burgundy. Then put in the Brandy, the Maraschino, the Brown Curaçao, the Bénédictine and the Soda Water. Stir well and strain the mixture. Serve in a large tumbler with the slices of lemon, orange and the fresh fruit on top.

## CHAMPAGNE COBBLER

1 *gill of Champagne.*
2 *dashes of Old Brandy.*
3 *or 4 dashes of Plain Syrup.*
1 *or 2 dashes of Lemon Juice.*
1 *dash of Lemon Peel Juice.*
2 *slices of Lemon.*
$\frac{1}{2}$ *tumblerful of broken Ice.*
$\frac{1}{2}$ *bar-glassful of broken Ice.*

This drink is prepared in exactly the same way as the Moselle Cobbler except that Champagne is used instead of Moselle.

A very refreshing drink.

## CHAMPAGNE CUP

1 *bottle of Champagne.*
$\frac{1}{4}$ *gill of Plain Syrup.*
$\frac{1}{2}$ *gill of Brandy.*
$\frac{1}{3}$ *gill of Yellow Chartreuse.*
$\frac{1}{4}$ *gill of Maraschino.*

3 *slices of Lemon.*
3 *slices of Orange.*
3 *slices of Cucumber.*
*Slices of fresh Fruit.*
2 *or* 3 *sprigs of Mint.*
1 *bottle of Soda Water.*
1 *big lump of Ice.*

Put the lump of ice into a large bowl and add
the Champagne. Then put in the Brandy, the
Yellow Chartreuse, the Maraschino, the Plain
Syrup and the Soda Water. Stir well and
strain the mixture. Serve in a large tumbler
with the slices of lemon, orange, cucumber,
sprigs of mint and the fresh fruit on top.

Some people prefer to use Brown Curaçao in
place of the Yellow Chartreuse.


## CIDER CUP

1 *large bottle of Cider.*
⅓ *gill of Brown Curaçao.*
¼ *gill of Maraschino.*
½ *gill of Brandy.*
¾ *gill of Pale Sherry.*
1 *teaspoonful of Lemon Juice.*
2 *or* 3 *slices of Lemon.*
2 *or* 3 *slices of Orange.*
*Slices of fresh Fruit.*
2 *sprigs of Mint.*
1 *big lump of Ice.*

Put the piece of ice into a large bowl and add the Cider. Then put in the Brown Curaçao, the Maraschino, the Brandy, the Pale Sherry and the Lemon Juice. Stir well and strain the mixture. Serve in a large tumbler with the slices of lemon, orange, fresh fruit and the sprigs of mint on top.

### CLARET CUP

1 *quart of Claret.*

¼ *gill of Lemon Juice.*

½ *gill of Brandy.*

⅓ *gill of Brown Curaçao.*

¼ *gill of Maraschino.*

¼ *gill of Plain Syrup.*

3 *slices of Lemon.*

2 *slices of Orange.*

1 *slice of Cucumber.*

*Slices of fresh Fruit.*

1 *bottle of Soda Water.*

1 *big lump of Ice.*

Make up in exactly the same way as Champagne Cup but use Claret in place of Champagne. Also add the Lemon juice.

This cup is very popular indeed.

## CLUB COOLER

⅓ *gill of Italian Vermouth.*
⅙ *gill of Grenadine Syrup.*
1 *dash of Lemon Juice.*
1 *dash of Lemon Peel Juice.*
½ *pint of Soda Water.*
1 *lump of Ice.*

Put the lump of ice in a tall glass. Then add the Italian Vermouth, the Lemon Juice, the Grenadine Syrup and the Soda Water. Stir well and serve with a dash of lemon peel juice on top.

A very popular drink.

## EGG NOGG

1 *teaspoonful of Sugar.*
⅔ *gill of Brandy.*
1 *dash of Rum.*
1 *Egg.*
1 *dash of grated Nutmeg.*
¾ *gill of Milk.*
½ *shakerful of broken Ice.*

Half fill the shaker with broken ice and add the sugar. Then add the egg, the Rum, the Brandy and the milk. Shake well and pass through a strainer into a tumbler. Serve with a dash of nutmeg on top.

This recipe can be varied by using Gin, or Rum, or Whisky in place of the Brandy.

## GIN CRUSTA

½ gill of Gin.
⅛ gill of Lemon Juice.
1 teaspoonful of Plain Syrup.
1 teaspoonful of Maraschino.
1 dash of Orange Bitters.
1 dash of Angostura Bitters.
The peel of a Lemon cut spiral fashion.
Slices of Fruit.
½ teaspoonful of powdered Sugar.
½ shakerful of broken Ice.

Prepare in exactly the same way as for Brandy
Crusta but use Gin instead of Brandy.

If preferred use Pineapple Syrup in place of
Maraschino.


## GIN DAISY

½ gill of Gin.
⅛ gill of Lemon Juice.
⅛ gill of Grenadine Syrup.
Slices of fresh Fruit.
Soda Water.
½ shakerful of broken Ice.

This drink is prepared in exactly the same way
as Brandy Daisy except that the Lime juice is
omitted and that the Gin is used in place of
Brandy.

A very refreshing and cooling drink.

### GIN HIGHBALL

1 *gill of Dry Gin.*
1 *slice of Lemon.*
1 *gill of Soda Water.*
1 *lump of Ice.*

Put the lump of ice in a tumbler and add the
Dry Gin.   Then fill up with Soda Water.
Serve with a slice of Lemon.

This recipe can be varied by using **Brandy,**
French Vermouth, Italian Vermouth, Port,
Rum, Sherry or Whisky in place of Gin.

### GINGER ALE CUP

1 *quart of Ginger Ale.*
¼ *gill of Maraschino.*
½ *gill of Brandy.*
2 *or 3 dashes of Bénédictine.*
¼ *gill of Lime Juice.*
3 *slices of Lemon.*
3 *slices of Orange.*
1 *tablespoonful of powdered Sugar.*
2 *sprigs of Mint.*
1 *big lump of Ice.*

Put the lump of ice into a large bowl
and add the Ginger Ale.   Then put in the
sugar, the Brandy, the Maraschino and the
Bénédictine.   Stir well and strain the mixture.
Serve in a large tumbler with slices of lemon,
slices of orange and sprigs of mint on top.

### HOCK CUP

1 *large bottle of Hock.*
¼ *gill of Kummel.*
½ *gill of Brandy.*
⅓ *gill of Yellow Chartreuse.*
¼ *gill of Maraschino.*
3 *slices of Lemon.*
3 *slices of Orange.*
*Slices of fresh Fruit.*
1 *pint of Soda Water.*
1 *big lump of Ice.*

Put the lump of ice in a large bowl and add the Hock. Then add the Kummel, the Brandy, the Yellow Chartreuse, the Maraschino and the Soda Water. Stir well and strain the mixture. Serve in a large tumbler with the slices of lemon, orange and fresh fruit on top.

Some people like to add, to the above, two dashes of Bénédictine.

### MINT COOLER

1 *dash of Crème de Menthe.*
½ *pint of Ginger Ale.*
2 *or* 3 *sprigs of Mint.*
1 *lump of Ice.*

Put the sprigs of mint in a tall glass and squash with a spoon. Then add the lump of ice, the Crème de Menthe and the Ginger Ale. Stir well and serve with a sprig of mint.

A very refreshing drink.

## MORNING EGG NOGG

⅔ *gill of Brandy.*
⅙ *gill of Yellow Chartreuse.*
1 *teaspoonful of Sugar.*
1 *Egg.*
1 *dash of grated Nutmeg.*
⅔ *gill of Milk.*
½ *shakerful of broken Ice.*

This is prepared in exactly the same way as Egg Nogg except that Yellow Chartreuse is used in place of Rum.

## MOSELLE COBBLER

1 *gill of Moselle.*
2 *dashes of Old Brandy.*
3 *or 4 dashes of Plain Syrup.*
1 *or 2 dashes of Lemon Juice.*
1 *dash of Lemon Peel Juice.*
2 *slices of Lemon.*
½ *tumblerful of broken Ice.*
½ *bar-glassful of broken Ice.*

Half fill the bar-glass with broken ice and add the Moselle. Then add the Lemon juice, the Plain Syrup and the Old Brandy. Stir up and pass through a strainer into a tumbler half full of broken ice. Serve with a dash of lemon peel juice, 2 slices of lemon and straws.

This is a long drink and is very refreshing.

## MOSELLE CUP

1 *large bottle of Moselle.*
¼ *gill of Kummel.*
½ *gill of Brandy.*
⅓ *gill of Yellow Chartreuse.*
¼ *gill of Maraschino.*
3 *slices of Lemon.*
3 *slices of Orange.*
*Slices of fresh Fruit.*
2 *or* 3 *sprigs of Mint.*
1 *pint of Soda Water.*
1 *big lump of Ice.*

Prepare in exactly the same way as Hock Cup but use Moselle in place of Hock.

If desired, add a dash or two of Bénédictine and serve with two or three sprigs of mint.

## NEW YORK COOLER

½ *gill of Canadian Club Whisky.*
¼ *gill of Lemon Squash.*
1 *dash of Lemon Peel Juice.*
3 *dashes of Grenadine Syrup*
1 *slice of Lemon.*
1 *lump of Ice.*
*Fill up with Soda Water*

Put the lump of ice in a tall glass and add the Canadian Club Whisky. Then add the Lemon Squash and the Grenadine Syrup. Fill up with Soda Water and stir well. Serve with a dash of lemon peel juice and a slice of lemon.

Prepare in exactly the same way as for Sherry
Cobbler but use Rum in place of Sherry.

This drink is very refreshing in hot weather.

### RUM DAISY

½ *gill of Rum.*
⅓ *gill of Lemon Juice.*
⅛ *gill of Grenadine Syrup.*
2 *dashes of Brown Curaçao.*
*Slices of fresh Fruit.*
*Soda Water.*
½ *shakerful of broken Ice.*

This drink is prepared in exactly the same way
as Brandy Daisy except that the Lime Juice is
left out, Brown Curaçao is added and Rum
is used in place of Brandy.

A delightful drink.

### RUM EGG NOGG

⅔ *gill of Rum.*
1 *teaspoonful of Sugar.*
1 *Egg.*
1 *dash of grated Nutmeg.*
¾ *gill of Milk.*
½ *shakerful of broken Ice.*

This drink is prepared in exactly the same way
as Egg Nogg except that Rum is used in place
of Brandy.

This is a very popular drink.

### RUM PUNCH

½ *gill of Rum.*
¼ *gill of Lemon Juice.*
1 *dash of Brandy.*
2 *dashes of Plain Syrup.*
*Soda Water.*
½ *shakerful of broken Ice.*

Half fill the shaker with broken ice and add the Rum. Then add the Lemon juice, the Plain Syrup and the Brandy. Shake well and pass through a strainer into a large wine glass. To serve, fill up with Soda Water.

This punch is one of the most popular ones, but you can vary the recipe by using Brandy, Gin, Sherry or Whisky in place of Rum.

### RYE FIZZ

½ *gill of Canadian Club Whisky.*
¾ *gill of Lemon Juice.*
⅑ *gill of Grenadine Syrup.*
1 *teaspoonful of Brown Curaçao.*
*The white of an egg.*
*Soda Water.*
½ *shakerful of broken Ice.*

Half fill the shaker with broken ice and add the Lemon juice. Then add the Grenadine Syrup, the white of an egg, the Brandy and the Brown Curaçao. Shake well and pass through a strainer into a tumbler. To serve, fill up the tumbler with Soda Water.

A very pleasing drink of medium strength.

### SAUTERNE CUP

1 *bottle of Sauterne.*
½ *gill of Lemon Juice.*
½ *gill of Grenadine Syrup.*
⅙ *gill of Maraschino.*
⅙ *gill of Yellow Chartreuse.*
¼ *gill of Bénédictine.*
½ *gill of Brandy.*
¼ *gill of Brown Curaçao.*
4 *slices of Lemon.*
1 *slice of Cucumber.*
*Slices of fresh Fruit.*
1 *pint of Soda Water.*
1 *big lump of Ice.*

Put the lump of ice into a large bowl and add the Sauterne. Then put in the Lemon juice, the Grenadine Syrup, the Brown Curaçao, the Maraschino, the Yellow Chartreuse, the Bénédictine, the Brandy and the Soda Water. Stir well and strain the mixture. Serve with the slices of lemon, cucumber, and fresh fruit on top.

If desired you can omit the Yellow Chartreuse and the Bénédictine.

### SHERRY COBBLER

¾ *gill of Sherry.*
3 *or 4 dashes of Brown Curaçao.*

3 or 4 dashes of Plain Syrup.
1 dash of Lemon Peel Juice.
Slices of fresh Fruit.
½ shakerful of broken Ice.
⅓ tumblerful of broken Ice.

Half fill the shaker with broken ice. Then
add the Sherry, the Brown Curaçao and the
Plain Syrup. Shake well and pass through a
strainer into a tumbler half full of broken ice.
Serve with a dash of lemon peel juice, slices
of fresh fruit on top, a spoon and a straw.
A very refreshing drink in hot weather.

## VERMOUTH APÉRITIF

⅓ gill of Brown Curaçao.
⅓ gill of French Vermouth.
⅓ gill of Soda Water.
1 small piece of Ice.

Take a wine glass and put in the Brown
Curaçao. Then add the French Vermouth
and the Soda Water. Serve with a small
lump of ice.

This drink is very popular in France and is
an excellent apéritif.

## WHISKY COBBLER

1 gill of Whisky.
¼ gill of Brown Curaçao.
1 dash of Lemon Peel Juice.
Slices of fresh fruit (including Lemon).
½ tumblerful of broken Ice.
⅓ shakerful of broken Ice.

Half fill the shaker with broken ice and add the
Whisky. Then add the Brown Curaçao.
Shake well and pass through a strainer into a
tumbler half full of broken ice. Serve with a
dash of lemon peel juice, slices of fresh fruit
on top, a spoon and a straw.

A very pleasing and refreshing drink.

### WHISKY COOLER

*½ gill of Whisky.*
*2 dashes of Orange Bitters.*
*1 slice of Orange.*
*½ pint of Soda Water.*
*1 lump of Ice.*

Put the lump of ice in a tall glass and add the
Orange Bitters. Then add the Whisky and
the Soda Water. Stir well and serve with a
slice of orange.

A very refreshing and pleasing drink.

### WHISKY CRUSTA

*⅓ gill of Scotch Whisky.*
*⅙ gill of Lemon Juice.*
*1 teaspoonful of Plain Syrup.*
*1 teaspoonful of Maraschino.*
*1 dash of Orange Bitters.*
*1 dash of Angostura Bitters.*
*The peel of a Lemon cut in a spiral.*
*Slices of fresh Fruit.*
*½ teaspoonful of powdered Sugar.*
*¼ shakerful of broken Ice.*

Prepare in exactly the same way as for Brandy Crusta but use Scotch Whisky in place of the Brandy.

Some people prefer to use Irish Whiskey in place of Scotch.

## WHISKY DAISY

½ gill of Whisky.
½ gill of Lime Juice.
¼ gill of Orange Juice.
½ gill of Lemon Juice.
⅙ gill of Grenadine Syrup.
*Slices of fresh Fruit.*
*Soda Water.*
½ shakerful of broken Ice.

Prepare in exactly the same way as Brandy Daisy but use Whisky in place of Brandy and add Orange juice.

If desired, add two dashes of Brown Curaçao. This improves the flavour.

## WHISKY EGG NOGG

⅔ gill of Whisky.
1 dash of Rum.
1 teaspoonful of Sugar.
1 Egg.
1 dash of grated Nutmeg.
¾ gill of Milk.
½ shakerful of broken Ice.

Prepare in exactly the same way as Egg Nogg but use Whisky in place of Brandy.

This drink is very pleasant and very popular.

## WHITE HORSE DAISY

½ *gill of Scotch Whisky.*
½ *gill of Lemon Juice.*
2 *dashes of Grenadine Syrup.*
1 *teaspoonful of Absinthe.*
*The white of an Egg.*
*Slices of fresh Fruit.*
*Soda Water.*
½ *shakerful of broken Ice.*

Half fill the shaker with broken ice and add the white of an egg. Then put in the Lemon juice, the Grenadine Syrup, the Whisky and the Absinthe. Shake well and pass through a strainer into a large tumbler. Fill up with Soda Water. Serve with slices of fresh fruit and a spoon.

If desired, a dash of Anisette may be added to the above. This improves the flavour.

## WHIZBANG COOLER

½ *gill of Dry Gin.*
1 *or 2 sprigs of Mint.*
1 *dash of Peppermint.*
½ *pint of Ginger Ale.*
1 *Lump of Ice.*

Put the lump of ice in a tall glass. Then add the Dry Gin and the Ginger Ale. Stir well and serve with a dash of Peppermint and the sprigs of mint on top.

This drink is very delicious and refreshing.